Isolde Schmitt-Menzel

Fun with Clay

B.T. Batsford Ltd

London

First English Language Edition 1969
© Otto Maier Verlag, Ravensburg, 1967
Made and printed in the Netherlands
by The Ysel Press, Deventer
for the publishers B. T. Batsford Ltd
4 Fitzhardinge Street, London W.1
7134 2451 6

Contents

Foreword

Moulding is a very ancient art. From earliest times, eating and drinking vessels and containers for provisions have been moulded in clay and fired, and human and animal figures incised and painted on clay. Our hands enjoy playing with this plastic element. Shaping a vessel still has its fascination—the object grows according to laws of its own. So let us explore the secret of this growth: water, earth, air and fire are the elements at our disposal. But do not expect any definite recipes. This book only offers you suggestions for your own experimenting. Once you have set to work, you will learn from experience, and discover the delights of creatively shaping clay.

Clay

Clay is dug out of the earth, and is a cheap material even in large amounts, so we can use it to our heart's content. It can be bought in plastic bags that keep it moist and easy to knead, from hobby shops and potteries. For the purposes described in this book low-firing clays are required (firing temperature about 1,000° C or 1,800° F). The clay may be yellow, red, white or black, but the colour is usually altered by firing. For large vessels with thick walls, fire-clay is best because it is specially resistant. Clay remains ready for use, wrapped in plastic bags or cloths, and kept moist, cool and airtight in a dark place. Hardened clay, spoilt work and dry waste should be broken up with a hammer and softened in a bucket with just enough water to cover it. Spread a plastic cloth over the top and leave it to stand for a few days. When

6

it is moist through, it must be thoroughly kneaded, like dough, on a board until it is of the same consistency throughout. It can then be used as before. Actually, it is advisable to knead even the prepared clay thoroughly and evenly before use, to expel any remaining air. Any hard lumps, or pieces of grit, must be removed.

All clay work must be allowed to dry slowly and evenly: for the first few days under an airtight covering of some plastic material, which can be carefully loosened from day to day. After five days it can be left uncovered, but never near a source of heat or in a strong draught. If a crack appears in it, it is no use trying to repair it, it must be broken up, softened in water and remade, so much care and patience are needed during the drying period, which takes from two to three weeks to complete, before biscuit-firing (see p. 50).

A newly invented modelling product combines the properties of clay and other traditional plastic materials. Ready for use, light and soft and easy to work, it has the special advantage of hardening in the air. Mould it, set it aside, and in two or three days the work will be as hard

and resistant as if it had been fired. It can then be treated like wood—carved, filed, drilled, sawn and glued. It can always be used again. Hard lumps can simply be wrapped in damp cloths, while modelled figures should be broken up and left to soften in a bowl with a little water. In a day or two the material will have recovered its original soft, malleable consistency.

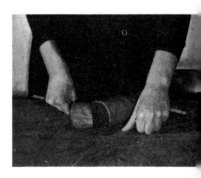

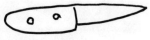

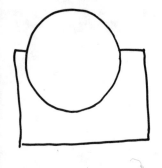

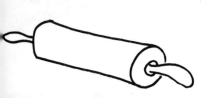

Tools

1 A kitchen knife for cutting clay strips (see p. 14), clay slabs, and levelling the rims of vessels.

2 A wooden board or piece of hardboard, round or rectangular, to stand the vessel on, leaving it to work loose by itself in drying. It should measure about 8×8 inches.

3 A flat strip of wood, about $2\frac{1}{2}$ inches wide, 10 inches long and $\frac{1}{4}$ to $\frac{1}{2}$ inch thick. This is used for smoothing the outside of the vessel while supporting it from the inside with the fingers.

4 A rolling pin for rolling out the clay-like dough on the board when making a mirror-frame or a tile.

5 A thin piece of wire for cutting the clay, 12 to 14 inches long, with a little wooden stick at each end.

6 A wooden modelling tool for smoothing the surface and incising decorative patterns.

7 A rounded plastic spoon, for smoothing curved surfaces in bowls and dishes.

8 Plastic bags or cloths for wrapping clay and unfinished work and keeping them moist.

9 A sponge for cleaning up the workroom.

10 An electric firing kiln. Some of the smaller ones can be run off the normal household electric supply.

If you do not want to invest in a firing kiln from the start, you can probably get your work fired for you. Many schools and institutes of arts and crafts have firing kilns today, and hobby shops and pottery studios will accept dry work for firing. Our illustrations show the ovens in which the small pieces seen in this book were fired.

Shaping a lump of clay

Boring a hole with the finger in a rounded lump of clay is obviously the simplest way of producing a hollow shape. The outside can be widened, and the internal space increased, by pressing out the walls from inside and outside with the fingers. Pressing them together with both hands increases the height, and carefully pushing them inwards will partially close the vessel. A little strip of clay set round the opening completes a rounded vase. Egg-cups and small bowls can be made in the same way.

Building up with rolls of clay

Pound a little lump of clay flat on the
board with your fist, and with some
round object—tumbler, cup, can—
cut out a circle to form the base of
the vessel. Then make a roll, about
12 to 14 inches long and $\frac{3}{8}$ inch thick,
of good moist clay and coil it on the
base, pressing each coil well down
on the last, so as to leave no gaps between them, and filling in the joins
inside with soft clay, smoothed over
with the fingers. To narrow the vessel, lay each coil a little further in, to
widen it, a little further out. You can
make a comical little cat in this way,
with paws and tail of a thicker roll
stuck on, and a slab of clay for a head,
with eyes and mouth incised or stuck
on.

Candlestick ladies

These comical candlesticks were built up with clay rolls, the faces being smoothed with soft clay. Each lady can carry a candle on her hat, and her arms serve as handles. Make sure the clay coils are firmly joined, and let the candlestick lady dry out carefully before firing her in the biscuit oven (see p. 50). After firing, paint the figure in part with black slip (see p. 51), pour a transparent glaze over it and fire it at a temperature of 1,000° C (1,800° F). A dark-ivory glaze poured over the slip will produce a light-brown mat mat surface, with the parts treated with slip showing dark-brown.

Building up with clay slabs

This method is particularly suitable for making angular containers, very large vessels or any made of fire-clay. Roll the clay flat, then cut out pieces of the required size and shape, but do not try to join too large pieces together or you will have a difficulty in welding the joins properly and they may crack in firing. The joins must first be roughened with a knife, and then thoroughly smoothed with

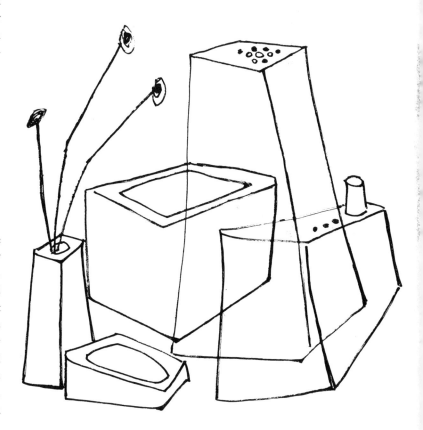

13

soft clay. The cover is fitted on in the same way, and can have holes cut in it for inserting flowers. This does away with the usual spike bunch arrangement and allows sprays and single flowers to be arranged in original, unconventional ways.

Building up with clay strips

Larger vessels are built up with clay strips, made from a roll of clay pressed and rolled out to a width of about $1\frac{1}{4}$ to $1\frac{3}{4}$ of an inch. Holding the roll firmly with your left hand, beat it with the side of your right hand to a strip about $\frac{1}{2}$ to $\frac{3}{4}$ of an inch thick.

14

Stand the strip upright on the prepared base, pressing it well down and smoothing the joins inside and out. Add strip to strip in this way to build up the shape, smoothing the outside by patting it lightly with the strip of wood, while supporting it from the inside with your fingertips. Widen or narrow the shape by giving the strips an outward or inward slant.

Tiles and stands

We can make a confident start with a few flat objects such as a simple tile. Begin by pressing, beating and rolling the clay out on the board with a rolling-pin to a thickness of about $\frac{1}{2}$ to 1 inch—thinner for small tiles, thicker for large ones. Cut out the shape of the tile—square, oblong or round—with a knife, and round the edges a little. If the tile is to be glazed, weigh it down with another board, wrap both boards, with the tile between them, in a plastic cloth, and leave them to dry.

This tile was decorated with a modelling tool. A good piece of work by a child.

Machine and tool parts were pressed into this very decorative wall tile. If the tile is to be hung up it must have a hole bored in it on both sides.

Cuff-links, earrings, pendants, necklaces

All these trifles are quickly and easily made.

Cuff-links
Roll out the clay, and cut out little slabs, square, round or oval in shape and about $\frac{1}{8}$″ to $\frac{1}{5}$″ thick. Dry them, fire them at 850° C (1,600° F), glaze them, and fire them again at 1,000° to 1,040° C (1,800°-1,900° F). Then glue them to cuff-link supports, which can be bought in hobby shops and elsewhere. Earrings can be made in the same way, and so can brooches, buying the glue-on clips and pins.

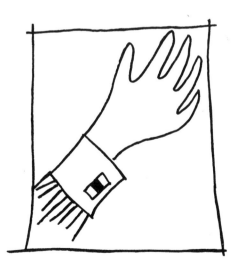

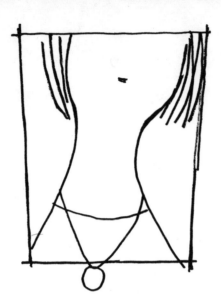

Pendants

Ceramic pendants are unusual and attractive in appearance, slung on a narrow strip of leather or velvet, obtainable in various colours. Glazing gives them a great variety of effect, especially if two or more glazes are superimposed.

Necklaces

Little clay balls can be bored through with a fine knitting-needle, fired in a biscuit oven at 850° C (1,600° F), and then painted in opaque water-colours —possibly in graduated shades: light yellow, orange, brown, or light green, ice blue, bottle green, dark blue. Brush hot candle-wax over them, or dip them into it.

Threaded on a thin silk string, they look particularly well wound several times round the neck.

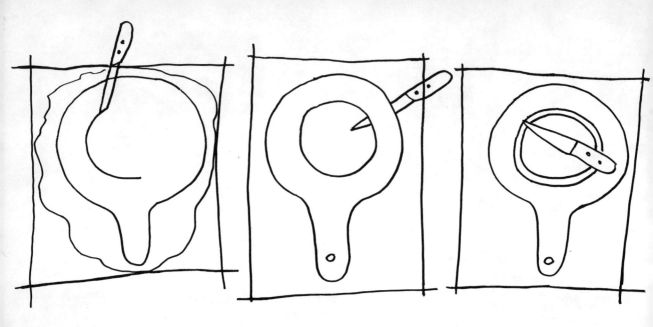

Mirror frames

Ceramic mirror frames are decorative and a little out of the ordinary. To make a frame for a hand mirror we must roll the clay out on a big rectangular board, to the thickness of ¾ inch, cut out the shape with a knife, and smooth the surface with the modelling tool and by patting it with the wooden strip. The frame must be left on the board to dry, wrapped in a cloth, for several days, after which it can be carefully detached with the aid of a flat knife. Smooth it again very gently on both sides and round off all the edges with the modelling tool. If you like, you can bore a hole in the handle to hang the mirror up by on a leather or velvet strap. Cut a flange at the back ⅜ inch wide to hold the glass. After the frame

20

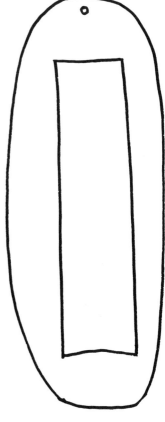

has been fired, glazed and fired again, a piece of looking-glass, cut to shape by a glazier, is inserted in it and made fast by means of adhesive and a strip of felt. The back must be covered with chamois leather or felt to prevent it from scratching the table or the wall. Round or rectangular wall mirrors can be made in the same way, but they should be made of fire-clay, which does not shrink so much.

The frame must be left to dry out, under a cloth, and then fired at 850° C (1,600° F), glazed, and fired again at 1,000° C (1,800° F).

Frames can be decorated with incised patterns or by the addition of bits and rolls of clay. A depression must be scooped out at the back for hanging them up.

21

Masks

A mask might be our next flat piece of work. Roll the clay out to the thickness of half an inch to an inch. If the mask is to be quite flat, the eyes and mouth can be cut out and the nose added on, but if it is to be semi-plastic we can press the clay up on the board to a height of 1½ to 2½ inches in the middle, and then model the features. After detaching the mask from the board with the piece of wire, hollow out the back with a spoon.

Flat masks are left to dry, covered over, on the board, till they work loose by themselves.

Hair, eyes, nose and mouth can also be made with clay rolls. In fact it is quite fun trying out fresh techniques.

Once thoroughly dried and biscuit-fired, the masks can be hung up as they are, provided we have not forgotten to make a hole for the purpose in the head or the ears. Masks can also be painted in water-colour and wax, or glazed and fired a second time.

Modelling animals

Working in clay soon makes us want to try our hand at little figures, and we shall find animals the easiest to begin with. We shall have to simplify their forms a great deal, however, because clay does not lend itself to making long, thin legs. We must learn to see in large surfaces, leaving

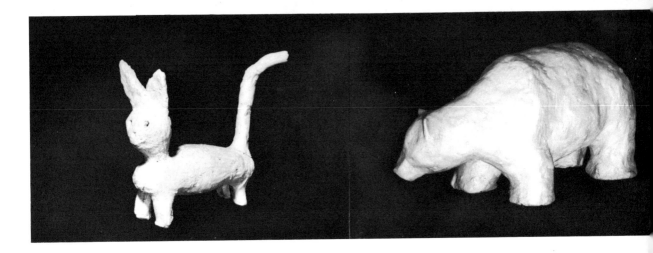

out inessentials. Ears, eyes and tails can be glued on, but legs, neck and head must be firmly pressed on to the body. Any large animal with a bulky body must be hollowed out from underneath with a spoon, to enable it to dry faster, and prevent it from bursting during firing; but with smaller animals, meant for a zoo or a farm, this is not necessary. The clay must be well kneaded, to expel any air left in it. When dry, the figures must be fired at 850° C (1,600° F). They can be left the natural colour of the clay, or glazed and fired a second time, or painted with water-colour and wax.

Built-up head

If you fancy trying a portrait of a relation, a friend, or anybody else, you can make a built-up head.

Begin by standing a strip of clay upright on your board to form the basis of the neck. All the strips used should be from ¾ to 1½ inches thick. Build up ring on ring, and at the level of the chin and the back of the head begin working outwards, gradually rounding the head and leaving an opening at the top the size of your hand. The clay must not be too moist, or the head may collapse. With your left hand inside the hole, use both hands to press and shape the head from inside and out at the same time. Add the nose, ears, eyes and mouth in relief with rolls of clay, and close the hole with a strip. Let the work dry thoroughly and fire it at 850° C (1,600° F).

Nativity scene

We can now make some clay figures for a Nativity scene. Any that have a broad base should be hollowed out underneath; narrow, standing ones are formed of rolls of clay. Draw eyes, mouth, hair and fingers with the modelling tool. Be careful to expel any bubbles, or the clay will burst in the firing, and, above all, let the figures dry slowly. We can add a lot of animals, made as described on p. 24.

Bird flutes

Bird flutes, whose shapes have come down to us from the folk art of many lands, are delightful toys. Children get endless fun out of them. Use a tumbler to cut out a round of clay about 2 to 2½ inches wide on the board, and build up strips of clay upon it into a tumbler-shaped object 4 to 5 inches high. Squeeze the open-

ing together and smooth the join well. Add tail, neck and head of soft clay and leave the bird to dry. When it is leather-hard, i.e. while the clay is still dark and easily treated with a knife, cut a flute mouthpiece in the tail and bore two or three holes in the neck (with four flute notes you can blow quite a little tune). When the bird is quite dry, fire it at 850° C (1,600° F).

The picture on the left shows birds that have been painted with majolica colours and fired a second time at 1,000° C (1,800° F).

Chess set

What about making a set of chessmen?

We must make them so that they do not fall over, and are easy to handle. After the first firing they must be painted first with black and white slip, and then with a transparent glaze. They are then fired again at 1,000° C (1,800° F).

If you want to make a chessboard as well, roll clay out to a thickness of ¾ inch, and cut out the squares to the size you want. Leave them to dry, weighted down by a board, and then fire them. Paint them, like the pieces, with black and white slip (not too thickly), and coat them with transparent glaze. Leave the underside unpainted, or they will stick fast in the firing-oven. After firing they can be cemented, like mosaic stones, into a table-top or a wooden frame, either bought or made at home.

Pieces for other games can be made in the same way, e.g. dominoes, draughts, checkers and so on.

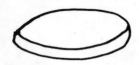

Piggy bank

A piggy bank is a general favourite. We must begin with a thick round or oval slab of clay, and shape a rounded body on it with clay strips, closing it at the top of the back. We stick on the snout, ears and tail and mark the eyes and nostrils, and then slit an opening for the money in the back—not too narrow, because the clay will shrink ten per cent in firing, and we must leave room for inserting the coins. As soon as the pig can be detached from the board, make four fat legs out of soft clay and press them on. When the pig is dry, fire it at 850° C (1,600° F). If you like, you can paint and glaze it and fire it again at 1,000° C (1,800° F), or paint it with water-colours and a coating of hot wax.

'Building' a town

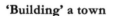

A little town with a lot of houses and towers is a delightful toy for a child. It can be a medieval town, a modern one or a village, made by beating lumps of clay into square or rectangular shapes. With a little skill you can beat the roof into shape too, or cut it with a knife. In our photograph the door and window openings were made with a modelling tool, but the walls can also be left flat, to be glazed and painted after firing—though they look just as attractive in the natural colour. If the houses are very thick through, they should be hollowed out underneath. Of course the town can have people, animals and trees in it.

Candlesticks

Never have so many decorative candles been lighted as today, so the obvious thing to do is to make candlesticks for them, tall or short, stout or slender, but all with a broad base to prevent them from overturning. Begin by laying an upright, circular strip of clay on the board. No actual base is necessary. Then build up the stem with further strips to the height required, and make the actual candleholder by stamping out a round slab of clay and forming it into a shallow dish. Lay this on top of the hollow stem of the candlestick and join them together by smoothing them from underneath. Form a spike in the middle of the dish to hold the candle. Another way is to make a little cup of one or two clay rings joined to a base and attached to the stem in the same way, taking care to make a smooth, firm join so that no cracks will appear later. Smooth the whole candlestick, dry it out carefully, fire it and glaze it. Incised patterns and imposed decorations in clay can be used to good effect.

Ash-trays

It is quite easy to make an ash-tray to please every smoker. Lay a lump of clay the size of your hand on the board and press and beat it with the side of your hand into a slab about half an inch to a inch thick. Cut a circle out of this with a round object of any size to form a base, and set an upright strip of clay round the edge, about 1 to 1½ inches wide and ¾ inch thick, pressing it on firmly and smoothing it well together. Then form at least one rest for a cigar or a cigarette, either by cutting a notch

in the rim or by joining on a support. Ash-trays should always be glazed, to make them easier to clean.

Salad tray

Even the kitchen offers many openings for objects made of clay, including a salad tray. This consists of a number of small dishes that can be assembled as one when laying the table. It can also be used for hors d'oeuvres or for different kinds of cheese. The individual dishes are designed to form a circle or a rectangle when assembled. They are made in the same way as the ash-trays, the rims measuring from 1¼ to 2 inches in height. Smooth the sides and corners inside with soft clay, to make them easy to clean. The number of dishes to be made is for you to decide. Let them dry very carefully and then fire them at 850° C (1,600° F). Coat them with leadless glaze and fire them again at 1,000° C (1,800° F). If you want to decorate them with a simple design, paint them with white majolica glaze and majolica colours, each dish with its distinctive pattern. A rectangular grouping has the advantage that it can consist of four, six or eight dishes laid together.

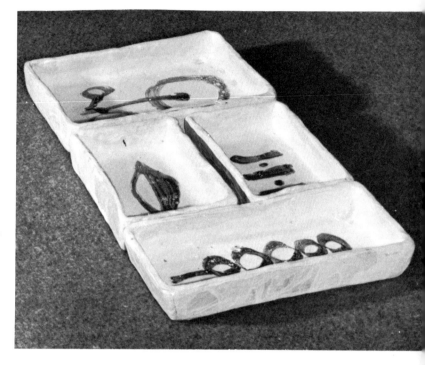

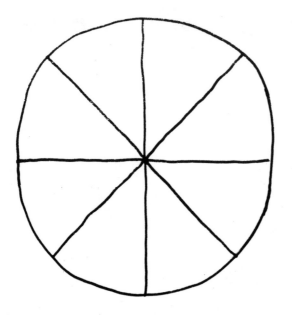

Dishes and bowls

To make a circular salad dish we cut a big round slab of clay into quarters or eights, to make the bases of the dishes, and then build each one up separately.

After this we can try our hand at a dish or a bowl. There are two ways of doing this. The first is to cut out a clay disk half an inch to an inch thick for the bottom and lay strips of clay upon it, leaning a little outwards from the start—the flatter the dish is to be, the flatter the strip. The rim of the dish must be reinforced. Tap the outside of the dish carefully all round with the wooden strip, and scrape it

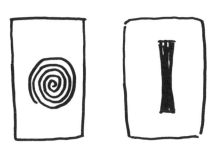

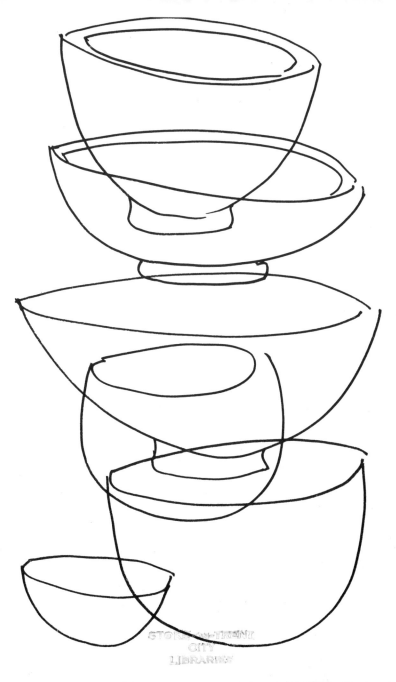

out inside with the wooden spoon, supporting the outer wall with your left hand. Turn the board constantly to make the dish round. The other way of building up is to begin with the rim, laying down the first clay ring the size of the top of the dish, and building the others gradually inwards till the opening is the right size for inserting the base. A thick roll of clay is then added by way of a foot. The dish must be left to dry for a day before turning it over and smoothing the inside. It must be covered while drying out, then fired and glazed. If the inside is coated with majolica glaze it can be painted with majolica colours.

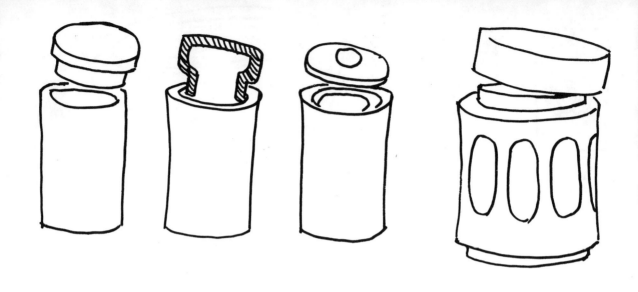

Jars

Jars come in useful for all sorts of things: cigarettes, biscuits, trinkets and so on.

A round slab of clay is again the first step, on which we build an upright cylinder, after reckoning the exact height it should have to take the contents, and adding ten per cent to this to allow for shrinkage in firing. The walls of the jar must not be too thin. A small strip of clay must be added to the inside of the rim to hold the lid and prevent it from falling off. The lid is made on the same principle as a cup, and tested for fitting. It must not fit too closely or it may stick. A simpler way is to make the lid of a clay disc $\frac{3}{8}$ inch thick with a little clay strip underneath to hold it safely on the jar.

Decorations, impressed and incised

These jars, like all upright cylindrical objects, lend themselves particularly well to incised and impressed decoration. The depressions can be made with modelling tools, nails or pointed sticks, working with care while the clay is still soft. If it is too hard, designs can be scratched in it with a nail or a nail-file. It is important to choose simple designs—circles, rectangles and lines for preference. The jars should only be glazed inside, or if coated on the outside, the glaze should be rubbed off the raised surfaces and left only in the depressions, producing a very attractive effect. The work must be finally refired at 1,000° C (1,800° F).

Big and little vases

Fire-clay is best for making these. We start as before with a clay slab as a base, taking care from the first to see that the outside of the vase is free from pits and unevennesses, and beating the surface regularly all round with the wooden strip. If the vase is to taper upwards, the clay strips must slant inwards. All vases should be reasonably wide at the bottom to prevent them from falling over. Asymetrical shapes have a charm of their own. Vases should be glazed in subdued colours—grey, brown, white or black—so as not to detract from the colour effect of the flowers they are to contain.

These vases have been biscuit-fired, but are still unglazed

This vase was glazed with a white vulcanite glaze

Jugs

If we add a handle to a vase we get a jug. The handle is made of a clay strip moulded to the right shape and firmly pressed on, the join being smoothed with clay. The handle should be rather thicker at the join to prevent it from breaking off. If the jug is to have a lip for pouring, press the rim outwards with the left forefinger, while holding it with the right forefinger and thumb. Leave the jug to dry, wrapped in a cloth, and after the first firing, glaze it and fire it again. We might make some cups to go with it.

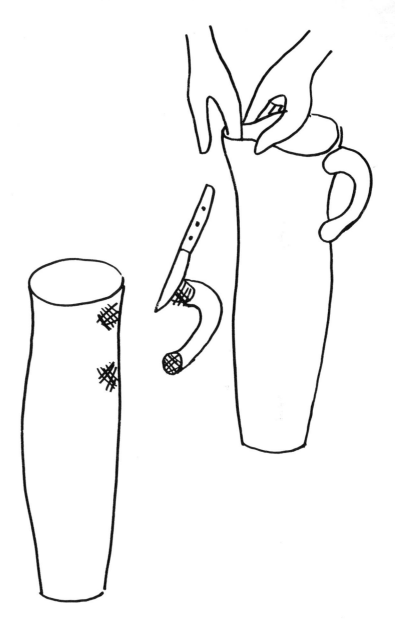

43

Fondue pan

To make a pan for a fondue we must use fire-resisting clay, and specify this when buying it. It can be obtained in powder form.

The powder must be mixed with water (instructions are usually given with the packet). In some cases ordinary clay can be substituted, provided it is mixed with a little sand, but the pan must not be placed over too hot a flame when cooking with it, or allowed to cool too suddenly.

The base should be fairly large—6 to 7 inches in diameter—and the sides about $3\frac{1}{2}$ to 4 inches high, built up out of clay strips. A straight handle is attached, and the pan is left to dry with care. It is then fired at 850° C (1,600° F), glazed and fired again at 1,000° C (1,800° F).

Tea-service

Now that we have acquired a little skill in shaping things, we might try our hand at a tea service. It should be as simple as possible in form. The teapot in our illustration stands solidly on its broad base. The cups are made on the same principle as the dishes on p. 36, patiently smoothed outside and in.

The body of the teapot is built up with clay strips narrowing inwards toward the top. The lid is flat, but has a wide clay strip inside, to prevent it from falling out when the teapot is tilted up.

The spout is made of a medium-

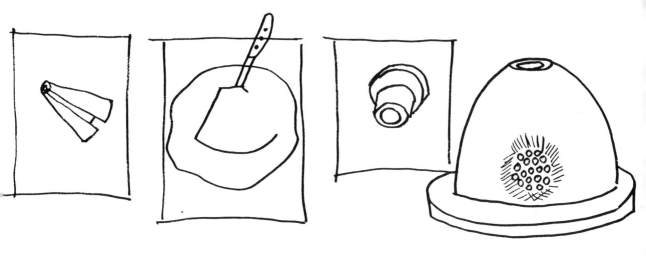

thick slab, cut out and shaped over the finger. The spot where it is to be joined on must be roughened with a knife, and the join itself smoothed with soft clay. The handle is set on in the same way. It is made of a rectangular slab of clay rolled up. The tea-service must be left to dry, covered up, and then fired and glazed. The service shown was glazed white inside and dull brown outside, and finally fired at 1040° C (1,900° F). A sugar bowl and cream-jug can be made to match.

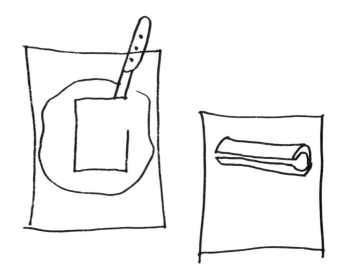

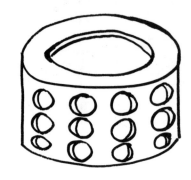

Small stove

We might make a stove to match the teapot by cutting out a round slab of clay 6 to 9 inches across and ¾ inch thick, and building up clay strips upon it to form an upright cylinder 3½ to 4 inches high. To allow air to reach the candle inside, cut ornamental openings in the cylinder with a knife. On another board, roll out clay to make a cover, cut to the same size as the cylinder; cut out a circle in the middle of this, and put a clay strip ¾ inch wide on the underside to hold it in place.

We can make the stove in another, easier way, by building the cylinder $1\frac{1}{4}$ to $1\frac{3}{4}$ inches taller, with ornamental openings as before, and notches $1\frac{3}{4}$ inches deep cut at intervals of $1\frac{1}{2}$ inches round the rim. Bend inwards every other strip thus formed, to make a platform for the teapot, while the upstanding ones, somewhat shortened, will prevent it from slipping off. The stove must be dried out, biscuit-fired, glazed to match the tea-service, and fired again at $1,000°$ C ($1,800°$ F). The cut-out patterns will be more effective if white glaze is used.

Biscuit-firing

After drying out for two or three weeks the work will be ready for biscuit-firing, which is done at a temperature of 850° C (1,600° F). The pieces must be placed close together, but not in contact with the sides of the oven. In a fairly large oven we can insert shelves on supports for more economic ranging in tiers.

Open the bottom and side dampers, switch the oven to stage I, and fire for about an hour up to 100° C (212° F). Then close the bottom damper and switch to stage II, firing for 2 to 3 hours up to 400° or 500° C (750° to 900° F). At 600° C (1,100° F) close the side dampers. Switch to stage III and fire up to 850° C (1,600° F). If the work is not to be glazed, fire from 950° to 1,050° C (1,750° to 1,900° F). Biscuit-firing in a fairly large oven takes altogether about 5 to 7 hours, and cooling 16 hours, after which the oven can be opened and emptied.

The temperature is measured by a special thermometer supplied with the larger ovens. Glaze firms supply Seger cones, which melt when the correct temperature is reached. This can be seen through the peephole in the oven door. They are supplied for all temperatures. These are all the firing aids we shall require. Everybody must experiment with firing for themselves, and keep a notebook in which to enter the result of each experiment, so as to be able to compare one with another.

Powdered fire-clay

Oven supports

Fire-clay supports

Trivets

Treating with slip

After the jugs, etc., have been biscuit-fired, they can be coloured in various ways, including painting with slip.

Slip is coloured, powdered clay, which can be bought by the pound in every colour. The powder is dissolved in water to the consistency of a thin mash easily applied with a brush. The patterns should be simple and subordinated to the shape of the object. The slip must not be applied too

thick or it will flake off. It can also be applied with a little rubber ball. When the slip is dry, transparent glaze is poured over the surface and the work is then fired at from 1020° to 1040° C (1870° to 1,900° F). If a vessel or a tile of red clay is coated with white or black slip, part of the slip can be scratched off again with a knife or the head of a nail, to show the red ground and produce a very attractive, decorative effect. In this case, too, a transparent glaze is used as a finish.

These objects of red clay were painted with black slip. They have still to be coated with glaze and glaze-fired

Painting with water-colour and wax

Another way of treating the surface is to paint it. We can do this if we have a little firing-oven of our own, or can get the work fired at a pottery, up to the biscuit stage. The paint is applied with a brush, and water-colour is the best to use, because it merely tints the clay without altering its texture. When the paint has dried the surface is given a coating of hot candle-wax, applied with a flat brush, or the object is dipped for a moment in the wax, which must be heated in a tin and used thinly and as hot as possible. This technique is suitable for the small objects we have described: masks, mirror frames, dishes, tiles, pendants, chessmen, piggy bank and bird-flutes. After cooling, the wax forms a water-and-dust-proof surface with a silken shimmer.

This cat was painted yellow, orange and dark brown, and then waxed.

Glazes

For our first attempts at glazing we might lay in one or two slips, a transparent glaze, a white majolica glaze, two or three majolica colours, and perhaps two or three coloured glazes. More than this would be too complicated. If our clay is red, as will mostly be the case, we must remember that the colour will show through any transparent glaze. If we want to obtain strong colours we must use opaque glazes or slip. White majolica glaze can be painted upon, as soon as it is dry, with ma-jolica paint stirred into a little water. The application must be neither too thick nor too thin. Tiles, houses, and the insides of bowls and dishes are very attractive treated in this way. We can order a sample assortment of glazes and fire little test pieces.

An attractive bowl
painted in majolica colours

How to glaze

Glaze is sold in powder form. Add it to an equal amount of water and stir with a whisk till it is completely dissolved, leaving no sediment at the bottom of the container. The brew must then be covered, to prevent the water from evaporating. If the glaze should become dry, add water, and stir it thoroughly again. Before using it, pour it through a strainer. Begin by rinsing the inside of the bowl with the glaze, and when this coat is dry, pour the glaze over the outside, either using a can, or painting it on with a wide brush. Small objects can be dipped briefly in the glaze. If you want to superimpose two or three glazes to obtain a specially interesting result, apply the first with a brush, pour the second over it, and add the third drop by drop. But the total coating must not be too thick, or it will run in the firing and make a

The way the glaze was poured over these vases is easily seen

mess of the oven. Mat glazes show up the earthy and stony character of the material, and so do brown and grey ones. Black and white glazes give prominence to the shape. When the glaze is dry, sponge the work clean underneath, or it will stick in the oven.

Glaze-firing

When the work has been biscuit-fired and glazed, it is ready to be glaze-fired. The bottom of the oven must be strewn with powdered fire-clay, brickdust or sand, to a depth of ¼ inch before inserting the work, which must be supported on one or more trivets, according to the size of the bases, so that they are slightly raised to prevent sticking if the glaze drips. In a large oven an upper shelf made of a slab of fire-proof clay can be laid on supports and strewn with powdered fire-clay. The different objects must not touch one another and must be kept half an inch to an inch away from the oven walls. The oven must be tightly closed and set at stage I, so that the temperature will reach 100° C (212° F) in about an hour. The bottom damper must remain closed during the whole of the glaze-firing, leaving only the side damper open. The oven is then switched to stage II and the temperature allowed to rise to 400° C (750° F) in about 2 hours. The side damper is then closed, and the firing continued on stage III to the melting-point of the glaze—usually between 960° and 1100° C (1,750° and 2,000° F). This firing takes about 7 to 8 hours. The oven takes 16 hours to cool, when the work can be removed.